# MARRIAGE IS A *Covenant,* NOT A CONTRACT

## *Glover Shipp*

 COLLEGE PRESS
PUBLISHING COMPANY
Joplin, Missouri

International Standard Book Number 0-89900-704-X

# CONTENTS

# STUDIES FOR SMALL GROUPS

Welcome to a new book series from College Press. The *Studies for Small Groups* series is designed for simplicity of use while giving insight into important issues of the Christian life. Some, like the present volume, will be topical studies. Others will examine a passage of Scripture for the day-to-day lessons we can learn from it.

A number of possible uses could be made of this study. Because there are a limited number of lessons, the format is ideal for new or potential Christians who can begin the study without feeling that they are tied into an overly long commitment. It could also be used for one or two months of weekly studies by a home Bible study group. The series is suitable for individual as well as group study.

Of course, any study is only as good as the effort you put into it. The group leader should study each lesson carefully before the group study session, and if possible, come up with additional Scriptures and other supporting material. Although study questions are provided for each lesson, it would also be helpful if the leader can add his or her own questions.

Neither is it necessary to complete a full lesson in one class period. If the discussion is going well, don't feel that you have to cut it off to fit time constraints, as long as the discussion is related to the topic and not off on side issues.

Because marriage is so important to God, and so much under threat in our society, College Press is happy to present this new four lesson study in the *Studies for Small Groups* series, *Marriage Is a Covenant*.

# MARRIAGE IS A COVENANT

Both sets of my grandparents and my own parents celebrated Golden Wedding Anniversaries. In describing their marital longevity, they all observed that, for them, divorce was unthinkable. They entered marriage for life. And among their acquaintances, divorce was rare indeed.

Not so with their children and grandchildren, however. Aunts and uncles had divorced. Brothers and sisters had divorced. Both my wife's family and my own family are emotionally scarred by marital breakups. And their children, in several cases, have carried on in the same manner.

This is to say nothing of friends and acquaintances, and even of Christian couples. Among all of these I saw the same tragedy being played out. Marital discord and dissolution are rampant.

What went wrong with marriage in just two or three generations? I pondered this matter at length.

During 18 years of missionary service in Brazil, where marital infidelity is epidemic, I concluded that little or no emphasis had been given to the *covenantal* nature of marriage. There, a brief civil ceremony before a justice of the peace is required. Religious ceremonies are strictly optional. As a result, marriage is often looked at as nothing more than a civil formality.

And then I returned home, to find that this same attitude prevailed here. This essential foundational relationship for all society was being entered and conducted as if it were a mere civil contract, broken at will, rather than a permanent covenant made in the presence of God and with Him as its originator and chief witness.

Faced with the realization of how society has erred in its concept of marriage, for the past two decades, when I have counseled engaged couples and performed marriage ceremonies, the fact of marriage as covenant has been my theme.

The lessons in this course are an extension of my premarital counseling and wedding ceremony notes. If we take the biblical principles on marriage presented in the course seriously, eventually we may see a turnaround in the "merry-go-round" of broken marriages, serial marriages, and live-in mates. Pray with me that we may help those about us see that marriage is a holy institution — a sacred covenant — and therefore to be treated with the utmost care.

Glover Shipp
May 21, 1995
Oklahoma City

# MARRIAGE AS COVENANT, NOT AS CONTRACT

### TRUE-LIFE SITUATION
### Marriage in a throwaway world

We live in a throwaway world. When I was a kid, awhile before the Ice Age, my mother darned our socks. Eventually the toes and heels were a crazy quilt of layers of darning. Today? The least sign of wear and into the trash go the socks. Ice cream freezers used to be made of strong metal. Today they are plastic. A broken piece and out it goes! My wife and I bought one and used it just once. We discovered that the plastic gears were already reaming out. The same is true of cars and computers. They are junked quickly and replaced. A friend mentioned buying a magnetic car key holder, to hide a spare key under her new car. It didn't work. There was no steel there to attract the magnet. And computers bought four or five years ago are already archaic. Many toys don't even get through Christmas Day. Few things are meant to last. It may really be true that manufacturers build into all kinds of items what is called "planned obsolescence."

*The throwaway mentality of our age has affected our attitude toward commitments and relationships,* as well as to possessions. There is little brand-loyalty. My grandfather would drive only Fords. Today, car dealers must have a shopping mall of makes and models if they are to stay in business. Nor is there loyalty to churches as there once was. The mentality seems to be, "If it doesn't bring near-instant gratification, throw it away and try another!" This same mentality has also invaded marriage and family relationships. The first time something goes wrong with the relationship, it's out of here.

Oh, it is made so very easy to sever the marriage relationship! To facilitate the option of breaking off the marriage, divorce is readily available. Here in my city a commercial loudly declares, "Why burn up your money on an expensive divorce, when there is Budget Divorce — just $68.00!" Some surveys indicate that one in every two marriages ends in divorce. Along with divorce and partially attributable to its consequences, one out of every three children today are born into single-parent homes.

With the decay of marriage comes a parallel decay in the quality of the home and family, with disastrous results. School teachers tell us that relatively few of their students these days come from a two-parent loving home situation. The impact of broken homes is bad enough for husband and wife. It is traumatic for children.

This state of our nation has come about in part from the throwaway mentality, in part from our lack of commitment to anything at all, and in part from a false concept of marriage. *Many look on marriage as no more than a civil contract,* easily entered into and easily broken. Many more look on it optimistically, but with the out of divorce, if it doesn't succeed. "After all," they say, "God wants

> The throwaway mentality of our age has affected our attitude toward commitments and relationships.

10

me to be happy, and this one I married no longer makes me happy."

## BIBLE BACKGROUND
### Significance of covenants

Although in our society marriage involves a civil contract, this is only a part of the totality of marriage. According to God's Word, the marital relationship is really based on *covenant*.

What is covenant and what does it signify? In ancient times covenants were of three basic kinds. One was between equals, such as in the case of the covenant made between Laban and Jacob, in Genesis 31. After having been victimized time and time again by his father-in-law Laban, Jacob decided to slip away with his family and flocks. When Laban caught up with him, the sparks flew. Finally, Laban offered a covenant of peace between the two of them. A pillar was set up, to serve as a witness to the agreement that they would never again encroach upon each other's territory or property to do harm. There were even vows made and God was called upon to judge the one who broke covenant.

A second type of covenant was offered by the weaker to the stronger, as in the case of the Gibeonites, in Joshua 9:3-15. Feeling powerless before the awesome power of the advancing Israelite army, as it conquered Canaan, Gibeon's city fathers plotted to deceive Israel and its leader, Joshua. They dressed as weary travelers from a distant country, come to make a covenant or treaty with Israel. Once the covenant was made and the Israelite leaders discovered the deception, it was too late. They felt obligated before God to honor its terms and not destroy Gibeon. This was not a treaty between equals, but rather a petition by the weaker party, the

11

Gibeonites, to the stronger party, Israel, to place its people under the protection of Joshua and Israel's elders.

The third type of covenant was extended by the stronger to the weaker. For instance, a suzerain, or more powerful ruler would conquer lesser rulers and offer them peace and protection, in exchange for allegiance and other forms of support, such as financial and military. Such covenants were serious matters. They included a prologue which identified the powerful ruler; a brief historical survey, which reminded the vassal of past obligations; stipulations involved in the agreement; provisions for maintaining the covenant; witnesses to it; and blessings and curses pertaining to it. Many examples of suzerainty covenants are found in ancient records. If the vassal ruler violated the terms of the covenant, he could expect dire punishment from his master ruler.

*Covenants throughout the Bible were also serious matters*, so serious that God held guilty those who violated their terms. For instance, the Mosaic Covenant, given by God to the people of Israel, carried with it great blessings for obedience and a curse on those who ignored its requirements. In Deuteronomy 26–28 we see a long list of blessings for obedience and curses for disobedience to the covenant.

What happened to those who failed to fulfill their part in God's covenants? Hear what the Bible says about the covenant-breaker:

> Both the house of Israel and the house of Judah have broken the covenant I made with their forefathers. Therefore this is what the LORD says: "I will bring on them a disaster they cannot escape" (Jer. 11:10-11).

> . . . the people have broken my covenant and rebelled against my law. . . . Now he will remember their wickedness and punish their sins (Hos. 8:1,13b).

**Covenants throughout the Bible were serious matters.**

12

These and many other passages clearly show us that we dare not play games with God and His covenants. He never loses in such a contest; we humans always do.

Our Lord is always faithful to His covenants and expects us to be also.

Throughout the Old Testament we read continually of God's *Hesed*, His covenant lovingkindness:

> "But the lovingkindness of the Lord is from everlasting to everlasting, to those who reverence him;
> his salvation is to children's children of those
> who are faithful to his covenant
> and remember to obey him!"
> (Ps. 103:17-18, Living Bible).

From this and other passages, we are reminded that *our Lord is always faithful to His covenants and expects us to be also.*

### LESSON TEXT
### Marriage and its covenantal nature

How does marriage fit into the realm of covenant? Simply, it is the first covenant offered by God, the more powerful, to His human creatures, the weaker. Seeing that the man He had created was alone and incomplete, He formed a mate, not inferior to him or superior to him, but different. And, as the French say, "*Vive la différence!*" In a sense, then, God said, "Adam, I give you Eve. And with this blessing, I offer you a permanent covenant of partnership with each other and with me. I offer you the joys of love and companionship. I offer you my protection and blessings. I offer you children and grandchildren." (As a licensed grandfather, I'm glad the Lord made arrangements for grandchildren.) The Lord continued, saying, "I offer you the home, a haven of security in a sea of confusion. I offer you stability and intergenerational continuity. I offer you the basic building block of society. In exchange, I expect of you a permanent and faithful relationship to each other and to me. I expect you to form a new mini-society, in which your descendants, Adam, will leave father and mother and will cleave unto their wives, forming new and faithful building blocks for the following generations."

As with all covenants in the Bible, that of marriage fulfilled the formula of prologue, stipulations, blessings, curses, and witnesses. The Lord God, originator of marriage, witnesses the covenant, as seen in Genesis 1–3. Stipulations to the covenant include obeying His instructions, forming a new unit of society, being faithful to one's spouse, and bearing children. Although curses are not specified in this passage, they are implied. Violation of any of God's ordinances brings His punishment on the offender.

But someone may ask, "Does the Bible really call marriage a covenant?" Yes, clearly so. In Proverbs 2:16-17, we read:

> [Wisdom] will save you also from the adulteress, from the wayward wife with her seductive words, who has left the partner of her youth and ignored the covenant she made before God.

These verses show us that when the wife marries, she enters a sacred covenant with God, as well as with her husband.

And what does the Word say about the husband? Hear Malachi 2:14:

> . . . the LORD is acting as the witness between you and the wife of your youth, because you have broken faith with her, though she is your partner, the wife of your marriage covenant."

*Both husband and wife, then, obviously are partners in a holy covenant, insti-*

**Both husband and wife are partners in a holy covenant, instituted by God and made in His presence.**

14

*tuted by God and made in His presence.* In more archaic English, couples marrying used to "plight their troth," meaning that they were making a covenant pledge to each other.

How do you spell marriage? C-O-M-M-I-T-M-E-N-T!

Do you remember what God's Word says about the extreme folly of breaking covenants? This includes the covenant of marriage. "I hate divorce," says the Lord (Mal. 2:16). Who would seriously contemplate breaking a covenant-based marriage? Who would risk violating the "until death do us part" nature of the marriage vow? "You shall be careful to perform what goes out from your lips, just as you have voluntarily vowed to the LORD your God, what you have promised," says God in Deuteronomy 23:23 (NASB). The marriage covenant is serious, lifelong, and not to be broken. *How do you spell marriage? C-O-M-M-I-T-M-E-N-T!* Commitment witnessed by God and sealed by a vow.

Sakenfield, a Bible scholar who has researched carefully the meaning of *hesed*, God's covenant faithfulness, notes:

> Contemporary uncertainty and dis-ease about long-term commitments show themselves in many ways in the context of the decision to marry: the transformation of vows into legal contracts that lay out all rights and duties in advance; the advice to a soon-to-be-married young woman, "Don't worry, you can always get a divorce"; "trial" living together, in which each becomes afraid either to ask for or to offer commitment; marriages with specified ending dates . . . most of these alternatives rule out by definition the possibility of faithfulness no matter what. God's faithfulness in all circumstances suggests that our own commitments should not seek to know every contingency in advance.

If covenant-breakers have always suffered God's wrath, what can marriage covenant-breakers expect at His hands? He certainly is not a happy camper over those who break their vows to Him and to their mates. And what about the effect on children, family, friends, and fellow Christians? How much have broken marriages contributed to the dissolution of home and family? To the emotional delinquency of children? To the downward spiral of our culture and morals?

I remember a childhood game called stacking dominoes. We tried to see just how high we could go with them before they fell. Sometimes we would get really daring and try to pull a key domino out of the base without letting the stack fall. Never worked.

*Marriage is a basic building block of society. Pull it out and the entire structure of home, family, school, government, business, and church crumbles.*

In Brazil, where I served for 18 years, weddings take on an added significance. The rings themselves are called *alianças* (covenants) and are specially blessed during the ceremony. Brazilians have seemed to understand something our culture has lost: that marriage is entered into as a binding covenantal relationship. From the most ancient times, rings have symbolized eternity, represented things sacred, and sealed agreements.

In His wisdom, God intended for marriage to remain a strong and enduring base for society. As the stronger party in and originator of the covenant, He entered into an eternal agreement with mankind to guarantee the solemnity, holiness, and permanence of the marriage institution. We, as the other party to the covenant, must agree with him to maintain faithfully our end of the institution. Only then can we expect to return to a stable society, both in the world and in the church.

All of this is foreign to the world's view of marriage, which has

> Marriage is a basic building block of society. Pull it out and the entire structure crumbles.

become a sort of serial monogamy — one mate after another. But, as minister Jeff Walling said in a speech at the Pepperdine University Lectureship in April, 1994, "We must have marriages in the church that are different from marriages in the world."

> The Apostle Paul compares human marriage to the relationship between Christ and His bride, the church.

How does God look on the marriage relationship? One eye-opening description of the kind of marriage of which He approves is found in Ephesians 5. In that passage *the Apostle Paul compares human marriage to the relationship between Christ and His bride, the church.* The husband is to love his wife as himself. He is to care for her and protect her, as Christ cares for and protects His bride, the church. She, in turn, is to honor him, as the church honors its husband, Christ. This implies a deep and lifelong loyalty between marriage partners.

## APPLICATION
### Putting the marriage covenant to work

In order to realize this kind of commitment, the marriage covenant must be renewed from time to time, just as God and Israel renewed their covenant. On our 25th anniversary, my wife and I went through an entire second marriage ceremony, Brazilian style, complete with the exchange of new rings. Perhaps such lengths are not necessary to ensure the reinvigoration of marriage, but it just might be a wise idea to repeat covenant marriage vows to each other at intervals, perhaps in conjunction with wedding anniversaries.

Marriage is too vital a key to the very survival of our society and of the church to play games with it. Marriage is Covenant, with a capital "C." It really was meant to be, and is, "until death do us part." This is our pledge made to each other and to God. Nothing less than this will do in His sight. Nothing else will guarantee the sacredness of marriage as God's first and most lasting covenant made with His creatures.

# REFLECTING ON LESSON ONE

1. How does the "throwaway" mentality affect commitments and relationships in general in our society?

2. How does it affect marriage?

3. What are the three types of covenant mentioned in this lesson?

4. Which type best portrays marriage as covenant?

5. What elements made up the typical suzerainty covenant of Bible times, and how does marriage fit into this pattern?

6. How does God look on covenant breakers?

7. What do the passages in Proverbs 2 and Malachi 2 say about marriage as covenant?

8. What is God's intent for the basic relationship between society and the institution of marriage?

9. Why should marriages in the church be different from marriages in the world? How can we make our marriages different?

## 2
T W O

# GOD'S ORIGINAL DESIGN FOR MARRIAGE

### TRUE-LIFE SITUATION
### Easy marriage, no-fault divorce

My longtime friend and missionary colleague, Gordon Hogan, echoed well God's original intent for marriage in this observation:

> When Jane and I married 47 years ago, we vowed then that this was for life. We covenanted that the word "divorce" would never enter our home or marital vocabulary.

In our day of easy marriage and no-fault divorce, this sounds hopelessly old-fashioned, doesn't it? If it is, then I too am old-fashioned. Married more than 45 years, the vows my wife and I took were meant for keeps. We married for better or for worse, richer or poorer, in sickness or in health, as long as we both would live.

There have been times when it got worse, far worse. There have been times when critical illness made life extremely difficult. We have suffered reversals. We have been disappointed, gossiped against, misunderstood and falsely accused. We have lost employment or left it because of an intolerable situation. We have been bypassed for employment or advancement opportunities. Loved ones have let us down. In short, we have undergone many of the stresses that every marriage confronts.

> God offered marriage to humanity as a sacred covenant, not to be broken except by death.

Adding to these stresses was the arrival of four sons, an adopted daughter and a foster daughter, a long and expensive pursuit of higher education, low-salaried Christian service, 18 years on the mission field and a subsequent return to stateside Christian activity, still at a subsistence wage.

But on balance, there have been many pluses along the journey. We have enjoyed a deep love for each other, a close family relationship with our children, beloved companions in the Kingdom of Christ, and immeasurable blessings in His service.

Never, ever, despite the strains experienced in our marital sojourn, have we even remotely contemplated divorce. You see, we firmly believe that *God offered marriage to humanity, and by extension to us, as a sacred covenant, not to be broken except by death.*

## AN ATTACK OF HARD-HEARTEDNESS
### The downhill plunge of marriage

Of course, humanity slowly descended from this lofty pact with God, coming to treat marriage in an off-handed manner. By the time of Moses, hearts made hard by self-will demanded divorce. No, the wife could not divorce her husband, but he could divorce her. If she burned the lentils, she was out of there, perhaps even at the end of his sandal. If she displeased him in any way, she could find herself separated permanently from him.

However, from the creation of mankind on, this was not the kind of situation that God desired for couples. As Jesus explained in Matthew 19:1-8, because of rebellious hearts, God had permitted divorce, but "*in the beginning it was not so.*" In other words, Jesus returned us to the Father's original intent for marriage.

Some pick up on the "escape clause" in Matthew 19, insisting that adultery is an automatic justification for divorce. Some even say that mental or spiritual adultery, construed to mean almost any excuse for dissolution of the marriage, is a valid reason to separate. Oh, how we need to return to God's covenantal blueprint for this union of husband and wife!

## LET'S READ THE BLUEPRINT
### God's plan for marriage and the home

What was this blueprint? That society be constructed of basic building blocks called families. These families, formed out of a permanent joining of husband and wife, were to hold all of society together. They were to be constructed around the idea of a man leaving father and mother and cleaving, or adhering, to his wife. There was to be no triad of man and two or more women, even though polygamy was practiced by some in Old Testament times. This kind of arrangement was fraught with danger. Witness the cases of Sarah and Hagar in Abraham's household, or Hannah and Peninnah, in Elkanah's home. Witness the calamity caused by the many wives of King Solomon, as verified in 1 Kings 11:1-6.

*These two, husband and wife, were to be one flesh, not only sexually, but emotionally and spiritually as well.* They were to be forever two, but at the

Husband and wife were to be one flesh, not only sexually, but emotionally and spiritually as well.

22

same time one: one basic unity of society; two souls merged.

These two would build a fortress of security in a dangerous world, a fortress that would be a safe haven for the growing children. Family members would make peace, not war; calm, not turbulence. Children would have both a masculine and a feminine role model to follow.

> A loving but disciplined home would give the next generation its best chance for survival in a potentially hostile environment.

They would maintain a safe haven for creating and bringing up children. *A loving but disciplined home would give the next generation its best chance for survival in a potentially hostile environment.* No matter what might occur in our turbulent world, marriage was to provide stability and continuity.

These model parents, whether rich or poor, were to rear children in the "nurture and admonition" of the Lord. This would mean maintaining a consistent "tough love" level of discipline and an environment conducive to spiritual and moral development. In Moses' Law, parents were instructed to teach their children God's Way daily, as they walked, worked and worshiped together.

At all times parents were to be a positive role model for their offspring. As they set the right kind of example, their children were to model their lives after this pattern and teaching of their parents.

The parents' influence was not to stop with their children and grandchildren, however. It was to extend also to others. The family, as God intended it to be, was to have an open-door policy on hospitality. It was to care for others, teach them the way of truth and demonstrate loving concern for them. And this was not only for the benefit of those outside of the home. It was also to demonstrate to their own family what it meant to be hospitable, loving and caring.

This sounds like a heavy responsibility. It is just that, and should therefore not be entered lightly. Perhaps that is why the ancients (and even some moderns) left the selection of a mate to experienced parents. We Americans may be among the pioneers of romantic love or sexual attraction as a basis for choosing a life's partner. We expect, somehow, that an emotional high is sufficient basis for a successful marriage.

## MARRIAGE MORE THAN SEX
### Ingredients for a successful marriage

Certainly, sex has a major place in marital relations. Praise the Lord that He designed this intense and pleasing impulse into our makeup. Certainly, romance is important to a successful marriage. *But there is more to it than romance and sex.*

*There is communication.* The ability to commune with each other, to understand and be understood in a loving way, is essential to the conjugal relationship. Most marriages, authorities on the subject say, are maintained on a superficial communication level — mostly monosyllables dealing with survival. For instance, "Pay that bill?" "You need gas!" "Won't be home till late." "I've got a headache." "Your son skipped school again." "All you ever want is sex." "You're spending too much." We can all think of many more, can't we? Real communication, which involves listening and feedback, as well as speaking, is an art which requires time, experience and much patience, but it is essential to the success of any marriage.

> There is more to marriage than romance and sex.

To illustrate the pitfalls in marital communication, a wife one time went to her lawyer, demanding, "I want a divorce, and I want it now!"

24

He asked, "Well, do you have grounds?"

"Yes, a small acreage."

He paused a moment and then asked, "Do you have a grudge?"

"Only a dinky little carport."

"Well, does your husband beat you up?"

"Oh, no, I beat him up by a half hour a day."

A bit frustrated by now, the attorney asked, "Just what is your problem, then?"

She answered, "Would you believe we can't hold a decent conversation?"

*There is companionship.* God saw that His creature, the male, had no companion suitable for him. So He brought into being a mate that came, as has been said, not from his head, to rule over him; not from his foot, to be dominated; but from his side. These two were to be partners through life. They were to be best friends. They were to be companions, drawing ever closer in the bonds and bounds of marriage.

*There is growth.* As the two live and learn together in their unique life's experience, they are to grow in mutual understanding, wisdom and love.

*There is parenthood.* This is surely one of the greatest growth motivations of all, as we parents are forced by circumstances to grow in our ability to outthink, outwit, and both disciple and discipline our children.

*There is spiritual stimulation.* *Our homes were to be bastions of faith,* surrounded by unfaithfulness of every kind. *The father was to be the priest of the family,* or in current parlance, the family's "point man." He was to be the spiritual mediator, priest, teacher, guide and protector of his family.

> Our homes were to be bastions of faith. The father was to be the priest of the family.

His mate, for her part, was to be submissive to her husband's leadership. Note the word *submissive*. This means ceding to the other's leadership. This is not servitude, but voluntary submission, which has nothing to do with the current controversy over feminism. There is room in a family for only one mediator and priest at the human level.

In today's world, there appears to be little male role modeling or leadership on the part of husbands/fathers. God intended for him to be the leader of his family.

However, there are times, says Paul in Ephesians 5:21, when we must submit to one another. This includes the marital relationship. There are circumstances in which the sensitive husband will submit to the better judgment and greater experience of his wife. For instance, she knows more than he in various realms, such as the kitchen and the details of child care. And there are times when he ought to submit to her in social, sexual, and other areas of her need.

## MARRIAGE AS GOD INTENDED IT
### Permanent haven of security

*This, then, is marriage as God intended it from the beginning: a permanent haven of security* for the spiritual, social, and conjugal growth of both partners, as well as the upbringing of children in the knowledge of God.

How far we have come from the creation, but it has been to a great extent a downhill journey. The only possible way to overcome our "throwaway-marriage" mentality is to return to the rules our Creator laid down for us. These are not impossible requirements. On the contrary, they are reasonable and, if followed, will restore marriage to the place of vitality it was to occupy.

> This, then, is marriage as God intended it from the beginning: a permanent haven of security.

26

# REFLECTING ON LESSON TWO

1. To what attitude did Jesus attribute the breakdown of marriage in earlier generations? How does that attitude affect marriage today?

2. How can the "adultery" clause in Matthew 19:9 be wrongly manipulated to justify divorce?

3. How should marriage provide a safe haven for creating and bringing up children? What dangers are present for children brought up in troubled homes and/or homes already fractured by divorce?

4. What eventual difficulties do you see arising in a marriage based primarily on sexual attraction?

5. What part does communication play in a successful marriage?

6. Why is companionship essential to a lasting marriage?

7. Discuss the value of mental, social, and spiritual growth together as husband and wife. What may eventually happen, if either far outstrips the other in any of these realms?

8. What part can parenthood play in either the growth or deterioration of marriage?

9. Why is it essential, in God's plan for the family, that the husband be the priest of the home?

10. Marital submission is a voluntary decision. Contrast it with servitude. When should the wife submit to her husband? The husband to his wife?

# 3
T H R E E

# MARRIAGE UNDER SIEGE

## TRUE-LIFE SITUATION
### Is monogamy only a matter of convenience?

*Never in modern times has marriage been under siege as it is today.* We know where it stands. It doesn't. All too often it falls. More than 50% of all marriages end in divorce. Is there a family that has not been fractured by the breakup of homes of parents, children, or relatives?

The media, writers, and entertainers in general scoff at the "old-fashioned" idea of monogamy. Mack Lyon, writing in his book, *With This Ring I Thee Wed* (p. 14), says:

> A Donahue-Oprah-Murphy Brown-dominated society has thumbed its nose at those precepts [permanence and integrity of marriage] and prompted fornication and adultery in every form, so that now we are reaping the bitter fruits of AIDS and other sexually-transmitted diseases in epidemic proportions, as well as widespread and uncontrolled teenage pregnancies and a lot of other associated problems. More than 30 percent of the children born in the United States [in 1994] will be born out of wedlock and another 1.5 million unwanted pregnancies will be aborted. Can we survive it all?

Even the church is far from exempt. Decades ago, divorce seldom besmirched the reputation and influence of Christians. Our colleges boasted that their alumni were almost exempt from this societal plague. No more — not among Christian college graduates nor among our church members.

Why this plague of fractured marriages? *We have bought into the world's guidelines, rationalizing that we deserve to be happy and our mate no longer makes us happy.* So we shed ourselves of this "impediment" to our self-indulgence and search for that elusive "prince" or "princess" who will make us happy. We are under the delusion that marriage is no more than a civil contract, broken as easily as any other contract.

What we have lost sight of is that marriage is a covenant, to be entered into seriously with both the Creator of marriage and our mate.

With this crucial principle abandoned, marriage becomes a matter of convenience, legitimized sex, a social arrangement. And marital infidelity becomes increasingly common, spurred on by social pressure.

Now even psychologists are saying that, although human beings are destined to fall in love, "they aren't designed to stay there" ("Our Cheating Hearts," *Time*, Aug. 16, 1994). In the same article, writer Richard Wright notes that evolutionary psychologists are saying that it is "natural" for both men and women — under some circumstances — "to commit adultery or to sour on a mate." The writer goes on to suggest that there is biological evidence that both males and females are designed to stray from the other. To evolutionary psychologists, the fact of a couple celebrating 50 years of

**We have bought into the world's guidelines, rationalizing that we deserve to be happy and our mate no longer makes us happy.**

marital fidelity is a phenomenon far from the normal course of things for the human species.

> A merely physical or social basis for marriage desecrates its holiness.

With all of the pounding that marriage is taking from every side, even science and psychology, along with a nearly total loss of respect for marriage as covenant, no wonder it is going through hard times. *A merely physical or social basis for marriage desecrates its holiness*, reducing it to the weakest link in the chain that holds society together. The consequences are everywhere about us.

## TODAY'S SITUATION
### A modern marriage parable

To illustrate, let us pursue the life of a fictitious couple, Kevin and Katrina Korba. They started dating during their senior year in high school. Shortly after graduation, they set up housekeeping in a tiny apartment, without benefit of a license or a wedding ceremony. "After all," they reasoned, "everyone else is doing it."

They both entered college and worked at odd jobs. Somewhere along the line, they learned that money was required, if they were to pay their bills.

Then calamity struck. Katrina became pregnant. She decided, against Kevin's express orders, to have the baby. So she dropped out of college and several months later, a boy was born to them.

Kevin felt responsible for the baby, but was resentful of its presence. He was trapped into an added financial burden. Along with this, both sets of parents, as well as Katrina, were pressuring him into legalizing the relationship. He finally gave in and a quiet civil ceremony was conducted.

They settled into domestic routine, if not bliss. As soon as she could after the birth, Katrina went to work for a computer company, leaving their son in a day-care center.

Kevin continued to study, while working part-time in a convenience store. They were getting by financially, but just barely.

Then Katrina found herself pregnant again, much to Kevin's disgust. He blamed her for not being careful enough. With this pregnancy, she was quite ill and was forced to quit work early.

This strained both their finances and their relationship even more. By the time their daughter was born, tension was running high. Their marital relations were in a shambles. They were barely speaking. When they did, they argued over anything and everything.

Finally Kevin graduated and found a position as a very junior clerk in a law firm. One of his associates was a beautiful single woman, older than he and very sympathetic over his difficulties.

Sympathy soon turned to intimacy, as Kevin entered a liaison with his "understanding" friend. Katrina suspected something was wrong and when someone saw Kevin with the other woman, she confronted him.

Belligerent, Kevin blamed her for all their troubles and stormed out, clothing hastily thrown into a bag. Katrina initiated divorce proceedings. After the dust settled and turned into mud, the judge gave her custody of the children.

Never in modern times has marriage been under siege as it is today.

Legal battles went on for months. Although Kevin attempted to gain custody, the children remained with Katrina. Through all this the family was fragmented, with the children bearing deep scars from it.

Eventually, both remarried. Kevin soon divorced his second wife and moved on to a third. Meanwhile, Kevin and Katrina's son became a serious problem, rebelling against authority and in trouble with the law.

> Divorce breeds divorce. Broken homes breed broken homes.

Later, as an adult, their son replicated his father's actions and spent an unhappy life, in and out of various temporary relationships. Their daughter later divorced twice and lived with two other men. The grandchildren were torn back and forth between their parents. Some of them dropped out of school and entered the drug, alcohol, and sex scene. They, too, appeared headed down the same dismal path that their parents had followed. . . .

Some insist that marital infidelity and divorce leave no scars on their children. Not so! Broken homes break the spirit of children and greatly increase the chances of their falling down the same slippery slope of family disintegration as their parents. Just as the children of alcoholics or those of family abusers may follow suit, the tendency toward divorce appears to continue from parent to child, even when the children hate what has happened to their parents and to them.

This is a vicious downward cycle. *Divorce breeds divorce. Broken homes breed broken homes.* Single-parent families breed single-parent families. And the cycle continues, as it slowly decays individual lives and society's very foundations.

## THE TRUTH AS GOD REVEALS IT
### Marriage does not have to be shattered by divorce

The tragedy of it all is that marriages do not have to be shattered by divorce — not if we understand even from before our wedding vows that marriage is a solemn covenant, made with both our intended life's partner and God. And not if we realize that God hates divorce. Yes, He does (Mal. 2:16)! He hates it because it breaks covenant, because it breaks continuity in the parent-child chain, and because it breaks down the structure of society.

That word "vow" was mentioned earlier. It signifies another sacred act. Covenants are sealed by vows — eternal pledges of fidelity. Is it no wonder that marriage, being the first covenant in all of history, is sealed by the vows we take before God and witnesses?

Marriage is under siege. Some would try to convince our culture that it is a relic of another more naive age. Some promote the idea of alternate types of "marriage" or live-together arrangements. Some would ignore it, criticize it, and ridicule it. How could this be, when God instituted it? Do we dare affront the Creator Himself, demonstrating by our actions that we think we know better than He what is best for us and for society?

Just perhaps we have missed the way to marital stability. Just perhaps we have bought into the *Big Lie*. Let us return to God's way for marriage, while we still have a faint memory of what it can be under His guidance.

## REFLECTING ON LESSON THREE

1. Explain why marriage seems to be under siege in our present society.


2. Why has the church, too, fallen victim to the breakdown of marriage and the home?


3. If we lose sight of marriage as a holy covenant, what are some of the consequences?

4. Comment on the current theory of sociological evolution, as it relates to marriage.

5. Do you think the illustration about Kevin and Katrina portrays marital life as it is being practiced today by many couples?

6. What are some ways in which divorce scars the couple involved? And the children?

7. How does divorce breed divorce?

8. Why do you suppose that God hates divorce?

9. Explain how our marriage vows act as eternal pledges of fidelity within the context of covenant.

10. How can we go about restoring stability to marriage?

# 4
## F O U R

# BACK TO THE MARRIAGE BASICS

## TRUE-LIFE SITUATION
### Marriage has been cheapened

There is no question that marriage has been cheapened by today's society. It has been cheapened by premarital sex, live-in boy or girl friends, experimental marriages, serial marriages, marriages made in Hell not Heaven, marriages casually entered and just as casually discarded, selfish and abusive behavior with one's mate, the mad desire for personal happiness at all costs, unrealistic expectations about marriage, intense pressures brought to our lives by society, unconcern for the welfare of mate and children, blaming others for our marital difficulties. . . .

The evidence is in and it points to a severe decay of values and loyalty as they relate to marriage.

In this course we have noted that marriage in God's plan is a permanent relationship entered into through covenant with Him and with our spouse. This was His intent for marriage from the beginning. According to Genesis 2:24, there is a formula for marital unity:

"Leaving and cleaving leads to oneness. Leaving that which is comfortable, that from which we care and clinging to the other, not our own self-interest, makes us one" (Larry Bridgesmith, *Wineskins*, Nov./Dec. 1993, p.21). To make very certain that humankind understood the sacredness, permanence, and unity of marriage, its Creator had recorded in His Word, "What God has joined together, let not man separate" (Matt. 19:6).

> Jesus called us back to this permanence and oneness that God had always intended.

*Jesus called us back to this permanence and oneness that God had always intended.* Hardness of human hearts had badly abused the institution. Jesus therefore said, "But it was not this way from the beginning" (Matt. 19:8). In fact, He called all other arrangements for marriage and its dissolution an affront to God.

## PRACTICAL SUGGESTIONS
### Painting a better marriage canvas

Now if this is God's picture of marriage, how can we paint our own wedding canvas? Here are some suggestions:

1. Since it is too late to restore countless broken homes to God's intent for them, we need to start with the children who are undeserving victims of parental separation. Let us begin teaching all of our children the true nature of love, as God defines it. Ultimate love, in His eyes, is not *eros* love, which in the original Greek sense means physical passion. It is not *philia* love, or brotherly love, which is shared only with a few family members or friends. It is *agape* love, the kind that gives without thought of receiving in return. It is the kind of love God demonstrated when He gave His Son to us. It is the kind of love Christ demonstrated when He washed the

disciples' feet. How many homes would fracture, if all those living in it practiced true *agape* love?

2. Let us show others *agape* in action. If we do not begin to demonstrate to them a model of what marriage is meant to be, how will the vicious cycle of divorce ever be broken? *Our own marriages must demonstrate the marvelous nature of this divine institution.* This is not to say that our marriages are ever perfect, because they are not. However, marital and parenting love must strive to have the qualities described by Paul in 1 Corinthians 13: It is long-suffering, kind, not envious, not boastful, not proud, rude, or self-seeking. It is not easily angered. It keeps no record of wrongs. It rejoices with the truth. It protects, trusts, hopes and perseveres. It never fails.

Dillon and Patti Bayes, minister and church secretary in Talladega, Alabama, won a Happy Marriage Contest, as reported in the November 1993 *Good Housekeeping*. Their description of their marriage went like this: "We gave . . . when we wanted to receive. We served . . . when we wanted to feast. We shared . . . when we wanted to keep. We listened . . . when we wanted to talk. We submitted . . . when we wanted to reign. We forgave . . . when we wanted to remember. We stayed . . . when we wanted to leave."

Simply by practicing these principles of *agape* love, and that is what the Bayeses evidently practice, we can eradicate most of the relationship crises that arise, including those in married life. We can show the next generation (or generations) what real marriage is all about.

> Our own marriages must demonstrate the marvelous nature of this divine institution.

3. We can build our *agape* relationship through purposeful acts of unselfish love. For instance, no wedding anniversary should pass without a special time together to celebrate and to repledge our mar-

riage vows. The Israelite people needed to renew their covenant with God at intervals. An example of covenant renewal is found in 2 Chronicles 29, when King Hezekiah rededicated himself, his people, and the temple to God. In like manner, all marriages need renewal at regular intervals. What better time than an anniversary? No time or money for such a celebration, you say? It doesn't need to be an expensive occasion, but it needs to be celebrated.

*Agape* loving is not an easy task. It demands our continual attention.

The important thing is time alone with your spouse, to celebrate your years together. Rightly, sexual expression will be an important factor in this celebration, but certainly not everything. Loving consideration and remembering, mixed with a powerful dose of romance, can mean much to a marriage.

The important thing is to care for each other. Find how you can best express your love for your mate. Psychologist Miral James, Lafayette, Calif., said in *Good Housekeeping*, June 1994, p. 56, "I believe caring people have the potential to create a marriage that is for loving. Loving is lifegiving. It provides freedom and releases energy."

Agape *loving is not an easy task. It demands our continual attention.* Otherwise, it will be drowned out by our materialistic and self-serving environment.

"Marriage for loving" is what Dr. Joyce Brothers calls successful marriage. Long-term marriage is not entered into, nor does it decay into, self-serving or abuse of any kind.

*Marriage for loving — covenantal marriage — is entered for keeps.* Divorce is never an option in this kind of marriage. Differences will arise between the two, certainly, but none that ever draws the couple into a black hole of despair and divorce.

# A PATTERN FOR THE NEXT GENERATION
## Setting a marriage example for the kids

Not only should our marriage as Christians reflect these divine principles of covenant and *agape* love. It should also set a pattern for younger couples, and especially for those not yet married. In the Edmond, Okla., Church of Christ, where I serve as an elder, a church counselor prepares couples for marriage. Then, following their wedding ceremony, they enter a honeymooners' class, where the building blocks for a successful marriage are put into place. If your congregation does not provide in some way premarital and post-wedding orientation, remedy that lack.

And our children? They must be taught from their earliest years that marriage is a sacred covenant. And, of course, they must see that sacredness in our own marriages.

This teaching will include the idea of sexual abstinence until marriage, for premarital sex is one of the greatest causes for later difficulties in marriage. Couples who live together without benefit of license have far less chance of survival in marriage than those who entered the marital relationship without this "experimental" stage. Fifty-six percent of divorced Americans lived together prior to marriage, according to the *Janus Report on Sexual Behavior*. As the report worded it, "Good rehearsal, bad show."

Above all, this teaching of our children must emphasize that marriage, according to its Grand Designer, is *covenant*, pledged seriously with Him and with our mate, and entered into for life.

> Marriage for loving — covenantal marriage — is entered for keeps.

40

# REFLECTING ON LESSON FOUR

1. Who are the three partners in the covenant of marriage? Discuss the role of each.

2. What had happened to marriage by the time Jesus came on the scene here on earth? To what standard did He call us in reference to marriage?

3. If we are to rebuild marriage as a permanent institution, where should we start?

4. Describe the three levels of love mentioned in this lesson. What is the kind of love that endures in marriage?

5. Discuss the attributes of Christian *agape* love, as it is described in 1 Corinthians 13.

6. How can husband and wife best care for each other? In light of the biblical description of *agape* love, how can we create marriage for loving?

7. How can Christian marriage set an example for younger couples, youth, and children?

8. How does premarital sex prejudice happiness and permanence in marriage?

9. How can we go about demonstrating to the world a better way of life than that of "safe sex," condoms, and casual sexual liaisons in general?

10. Now that we have arrived at the end of this course, summarize the principle that "marriage is covenant" and the implications of this for your marriage and that of your associates.

# About the Author

Glover Shipp is the Senior Editor of *The Christian Chronicle* and member of the staff at Oklahoma Christian University of Science and Arts, Oklahoma City. Dr. Shipp received his B.A. in art and M.A. in communication from Pepperdine University, his M.A. in missiology, M.Div., and Doctorate in urban anthropology from Fuller Theological Seminary. He is an elder for Edmond Church of Christ, and an associate of The World Group, an international business advisory firm. He is an advisory board member for Helping Hands; on the board of the White Rock Fund, a missionary support group; and on the editorial board for *Power for Today*. He and his family were missionaries in Brazil for 18 years where he specialized in publications. Glover is fluent in Portuguese and moderately fluent in Spanish. He has been a staff artist for Good News Press, Dallas, Texas, the *Oakland Tribune*, and Dow Chemical Company. Space does not allow the listing of Dr. Shipp's many accomplishments and awards.

Glover and his wife, Margie, have four sons, one daughter, and one foster-daughter. They also have eleven grandchildren and two foster grandchildren. Margie is in charge of student records at Oklahoma Christian University.

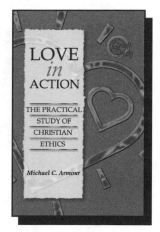

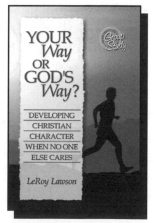
*(To order, see the next page)*

# What Men Need to Hear:
## Becoming God's Spiritual Leader
## through Moral Strength
### *Rick Atchley*

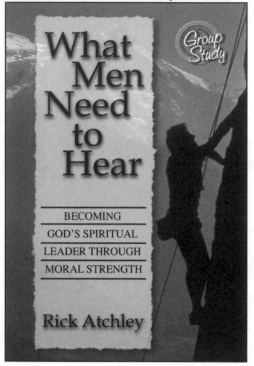

The moral character of the world runs contrary to the standards of spiritual morality revealed in the Scriptures. God needs spiritual leaders now. Integrity, purity, and holiness are the challenge set before Christian men because that is what they need to hear.

90 pages, soft, #A20-826-7, $6.99

# Phone: 800-289-3300
# Fax: 417-623-8250
## E-mail: books@collegepress.com